Helping babies help themselves
From in your arms to standing alone

Vickie Meade, PT, DSc, MPH, PCS
Janette Heath Osborne, DipPhys, APA
Drawings by Christina Frank

ACER Press

First published 2012
by ACER Press, an imprint of
Australian Council *for* Educational Research Ltd
9 Prospect Hill Road, Camberwell
Victoria, 3124, Australia

www.acerpress.com.au
sales@acer.edu.au

Edited by Elisa Webb
Cover design, text design and typesetting by ACER Project Publishing
Printed in Australia by BPA Print Group

National Library of Australia Cataloguing-in-Publication entry:

Author: Meade, Vickie.

Title: Helping babies help themselves : from in your arms to
                standing alone / Vickie Meade, Janette Heath Osborne;
                drawings by Christina Frank.

ISBN: 9781742860992 (pbk.)

Subjects: Child rearing.
                Child development.
                Parenting.

Other Authors/Contributors:
                Heath Osborne, Janette.
                Frank, Christina.

Dewey Number: 155.422

Foreword

Parents rarely have an opportunity to take a guided journey in learning how their babies move their bodies in the first year of life. This fascinating transformation from newborn movement to infant walking is beautifully described and illustrated by Meade and Heath Osborne with particular attention to addressing common questions parents encounter at each major stage. Strategies to help parents support their infants' posture and movement are highlighted in 'Quick Tip' segments throughout the book. The authors address potential movement differences of infants born prematurely and give expert guidance for challenges any baby may encounter learning to play on the tummy, balance in sitting, or crawl on hands and knees.

Another strength of this highly useful book is the brilliant discussion of how the movement of babies is related to emotional expression and to infant communication. This understanding of the interconnectedness of infant movement, emotion and communication can open new opportunities to engage in, interact with and enjoy movement experiences with babies.

I highly recommend this interesting, empowering book to all involved in infant care, especially parents and grandparents. You will develop new insights and new ways to take pleasure in and communicate with your baby. Enjoy the journey!

Jane K Sweeney PT, PhD, PCS, FAPTA
Pediatric Physical Therapist
Professor and Graduate Program Director
Doctoral Programs in Pediatric Science
Rocky Mountain University of Health Professions
Provo, Utah

About the authors

Dr Vickie Meade

Dr Meade received her doctoral science degree with a focus on screening four-month-old infants using parent concerns and the *Meade Movement Checklist* in a two-step process. Dr Meade is a board-certified clinical specialist in pediatric physical therapy, with a Master of Public Health in Maternal and Child Health. Dr Meade is currently active in research on early screening and innovative service delivery models for infants, young children and their families. Dr Meade has been teaching courses related to early screening and intervention for over twenty years, as Adjunct Professor in the Master of Physical Therapy Program at St Catherine University, Minnesota (St Paul Campus), at Seattle Pacific University and internationally. Dr Meade's publications include *Partners in movement: A family centered approach to pediatric kinesiology* and *Handwriting: Anatomy of a collaborative assessment/intervention model* with Rhoda Erhardt.

Janette Heath Osborne

Physiotherapist Janette Heath Osborne has had over twenty-five years of clinical involvement with infants and their families. She has worked in Sydney, and at The Portland Hospital for Women and Children in London. At the University of Sydney she became clinical supervisor then lecturer at the School of Physiotherapy, Camperdown. Later, while chief physiotherapist at the Crown Street Women's Hospital, she was visiting lecturer at Cumberland College, Lidcombe. At Crown Street, Janette worked in the intensive care unit and started the growth and development follow-up clinic, with Vickie Meade and psychologists Dr Robyn Dolby and Beulah Warren. This team carried out a clinical trial for a group of low-birth-weight infants and their families over the first year of life from Crown Street and The Royal Hospital for Women, Paddington.

For the following ten years Janette worked with Beulah Warren for the Benevolent Society of New South Wales in the home-based Early Intervention Programme for the prevention of child abuse and neglect. She is currently active in continuing her interest in mothers and babies, working with early childhood nurse specialists in Sydney.

Christina Frank

Christina has always loved to draw, paint and make things. She studied architecture and worked as an architect for a number of years. Since then she has had three boys (all of whom she assiduously wrapped), run an after-school art program, and started sculpting in clay. She lives on a wild block on Sydney's Northern Beaches with her husband, teenage sons and their large dog.

Acknowledgements

Thank you to Jann Zintgraff and Marianne Nicholson, nurse specialists in early childhood health in the eastern suburbs of Sydney, for their support and encouragement and editing advice, and suggestions for content in the first draft of this publication.

Thanks to psychologists Dr Robyn Dolby and Beulah Warren, who worked with us to start the follow-up clinic for premature infants at the Crown Street Women's Hospital and again at The Royal Hospital for Women, Paddington; and The Early Infancy Project with premature infants. Thank you for your influence and for guiding our work with babies and mothers over many years.

Thank you to Helen Hardy, occupational therapist at Westmead Hospital, for providing suggestions on the content and writing of the first draft of the manual. Thank you for giving your wisdom and long experience for the caring of premature infants.

Thank you to the parents for their generous contribution of time to allow the artist Christina Frank to complete her illustrations.

Finally, we acknowledge that most of what we know about babies, we have learned from the infants!

Contents

A note to parents

Congratulations, you have welcomed a new addition to your life! Your role as a parent is to help your baby master tasks that you are naturally 'tuned' to do together. Your infant will learn about the world through you and you will learn about your baby's innate temperament and motor skills. His sense of himself will expand during the experiences he enjoys with you. These experiences will motivate him to try harder and harder tasks over his first year.

But like us all, babies need help and encouragement to enjoy each stage in development. In this book, we look at what is going on for your infant and how you can help. We offer simple ways you can observe and become aware of your baby's attempts to master each step. The process of trying, then taking breaks, reflects your baby's first experiences of motor skills. He will practice, refine and regulate them (similar to his use of emotional and communication skills), using you as a guide, a challenger and a cheer squad. Your baby's progress is a process for you both to take pleasure in.

Note: In this book 'he' and 'she' are used in alternate chapters to talk about a child.

An illustrated guide

This book shows how your baby moves from a 'curled in' newborn to a standing youngster with a growing sense of independence. We describe the usual progress that takes place for most babies over the first year, integrating current researchers' points of view and highlighting the hidden details of each step towards the observable milestones of crawling and walking.

The drawings, photographs and brief descriptions illustrate four stages of development, which can be broken into the first three months, four to six months, six to eight months and eight to twelve months. The drawings will guide you as your baby practises building on each important skill and will increase your awareness of what he is working on so you can tailor your help.

The Quick Tips at the end of each chapter represent the authors' clinical experience working with hundreds of families during a controlled research trial comparing infants born early with those born at full term, watching infants with their parents, and together discovering what an individual infant is trying to do but finding too difficult. Each Quick Tip will get your infant 'over the wall' if they are trying to help themselves on to the next step.

Babies want to move. Your baby needs to strengthen his muscles to form the building blocks for movement. Strengthening these muscles every day helps him gain mastery over his body and limbs. Around one year of age, your baby will stand on two feet and look around at the world. A triumph of emotional and physical development! In time, your young child will use this strength to run, climb and jump against gravity.

As parents, you can watch and anticipate what your baby is working on and how he is trying to help himself. You can also become aware of when your baby might need a helping hand. This book will help you to appreciate your clever baby, to understand his challenges along the way, and to give him the support he needs.

Dr Vickie Meade   Janette Heath Osborne

Chapter 1

Your newborn baby

How movement begins

Welcoming a new baby is an exciting time! On arrival from the womb to this new world a baby needs and wants to feel safe, warm and secure. You are the one she relies on for help with her tasks of sleeping, feeding, watching and learning. Assisting your baby to soothe helps her with her tasks and cements the wonderful connections between you both. This chapter will describe the early movements your baby is making, and how you can help calm her after movement so that she rests more easily.

In the last months before birth, your baby exercised. She became more 'curled in' as she grew larger in the womb. She pushed out against the strong wall of the uterus and strengthened the muscles of her body which curl in and those which stretch out. After birth, from this curled (flexed) posture, your baby continues to use the muscles which straighten out (extend) the limbs and body and stretch the curled-in muscles.[1] It is important for each of these muscle groups to be in balance. The muscles which curl in become more active and balance the muscles which stretch out.

At six weeks, your baby is starting to kick out further, lie flatter and use larger arcs of movement. By three months your baby has developed control of the muscles of the head and neck. Your baby's vision is also developing so she sees further and becomes stimulated by her awareness of her surroundings. These new skills demand more emotional effort and self-containment. The beginning movements form building blocks for the active strength of muscles, which will be illustrated in all the movements of the four- to six-month-old infant.

What your newborn baby is working on

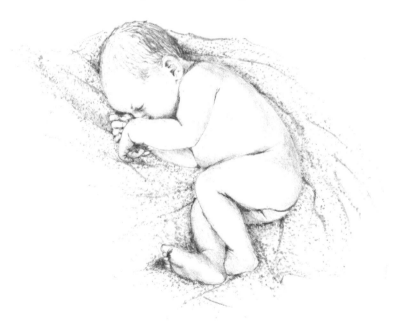

Your baby is learning to soothe herself and be calm and quiet so she can manage her first three tasks:

- to sleep
- to feed
- to awaken refreshed to look around and know you.

You will get to know your baby from her responses to the ways you hold, carry, look at and help soothe her. Your baby wants to get to know you, as you do her. She tells you her feelings through body signals such as facial expressions and arm and leg movements, and through emotions. Her emotions will range from calm and quiet, to fussing, and then, if upset, progress to loud crying combined with a lot of movement and activity of body, arms and legs. This emotional arousal has a strong connection to your baby's movements even at this young age.[2]

We all respond to our environment physically and emotionally. We become aware of bodily sensations and then adjust in ways that meet our needs. Physically, if we are cold, we put on more clothes; if we are tired, we rest. Emotionally, if something upsets us we may react by feeling angry, so we find ways to soothe and calm ourselves; we may have a cup of tea and sit down. We regain our equilibrium, our emotional balance. Newborn babies are the same. They use physical ways to help themselves manage their behaviour. If she is hungry, your baby reacts and shows her discomfort emotionally by crying, and physically by stretching out her limbs and body. When held, she responds physically by curling in with help from a carer's arms, and then calms her body so she is ready to feed or settle. This process of how each of us feels, responds, then calms, is called 'self-regulation'.

Curling in

Your newborn baby uses the curling-in position to help return to a calm and relaxed state of emotion, and she will go back to this position after being moved.[3]

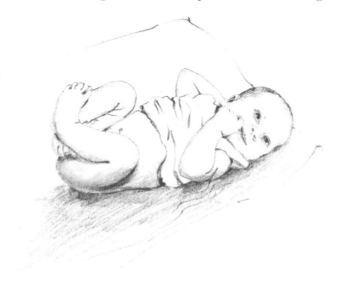

When you place your baby on her back, you will notice she actively curls her legs up and brings her arms close to her body. She curls in to be calm, still and ready to feed or sleep.

As your baby enjoys more time awake, she will also enjoy stretching out more when you change her nappy or dress her. Notice how her arms and legs straighten to move away from the centre of her body.

These beginning movements of curling in and then stretching out, illustrated by kicking of the legs and waving of the arms, form building blocks for the active control of muscles and for sensations of movement, which will become the basis for milestones such as pushing up and crawling. The muscles which curl in become more and more active as they begin to balance the muscles which stretch out. The movements also give the sensations which form the basis of sensory–motor development.

How Mum and Dad can help

Babies have an amazing capacity and ability to connect with their parents in order to master their tasks. However, newborn babies cannot manage alone—they need the care of their parents to meet all their needs. Babies connect with parents through contact which is enjoyable and reassuring. This enables babies to build an expectation of what contact means and what to expect from others.

All parents have times that they feel anxious when trying to meet their baby's needs. Just holding an infant has been shown by researchers to help the infant calm when crying.[4] But if you are feeling unable to calm yourself, then it becomes difficult to be relaxed enough to hold your baby in a way that helps the baby to calm herself. At these times, you may find it helpful to wrap and place your baby in her cot, or to wrap and carry your baby in a baby sling, continually checking on her response to being in the sling. Wrapping offers your baby a sense of being held by the swaddling cloth, and is described in the Quick Tip section on p. 12. The cloth provides a sense of contact. To feel comfortable in using a wrap effectively, it helps to practise at times when you feel calm.

You can help your baby keep a still, curled-in posture by the way you hold her. This will help her stop extra body and arm movements which might get in the way of calming and relaxing.

Some questions you might ask about the first three months

How can I help my baby control her movements?

You newborn baby uses 'curling in' and will return to this position after moving. Using this position helps your baby become calm and still. This position also helps her gain movement control by strengthening the muscles which curl the body and limbs in against gravity, and those that push the limbs out. You can assist with both of these tasks by helping her continue to curl in, and by giving her time for stretching out, such as when you unwrap her for dressing, changing her nappy, bathing and playing on your lap or on the floor.

Do babies find curling in difficult?

Yes, some have a lot of difficulty, and may take a longer time and need more help to return to a curling in of arms and legs to still movement. All babies need some help.

Does curling in help my baby settle?

Sometimes your baby may become overly tired and fussy. She may cry, kick and thrash as part of the way she tells you when things are not comfortable. Curling in is a comfortable position, particularly when she is tired. It is a familiar position from her time in the womb, and helps her become still and calm.

You can help your baby curl in and settle by holding her in a curled position and/or wrapping her. It is important to get her hips and knees curled up, and to round her shoulders and arms. Babies use their hands near their face as a comfort to soothe and calm, so when curling your baby in it will help to place her hands tucked under her chin. If needed, use a dummy. When your baby is wrapped in this position, you can place her in her cot, rock her or just have her relax with you. You can also use curling in when carrying her, lifting her or when wearing a baby sling. When asleep, your baby must be placed on her back, consistent with the recommendations for the prevention of Sudden Infant Death Syndrome (SIDS).[5]

Does curling in help when feeding my baby?

When a baby's chin is close to her chest, the muscles of her tongue and lips are able to grasp and suck. When her head tilts back, her mouth will open and swallowing is much more difficult. Supporting her head and shoulders will help your baby latch on to the breast or bottle more vigorously.

How does curling in help my baby look at me?

Due to reflexes she has from birth, your baby finds it difficult to hold her head in the centre and look at your face. You can help her overcome these reflexes when you gently hold her head forward with your hand, or by placing a pillow under her head when she is on the change table or on her back on the floor. Fathers in particular usually enjoy face-to-face interaction with their babies.

Why is it important to balance the strength of muscles that curl in with those that stretch out?

If one group of muscles becomes stronger than another it makes some movements more difficult. For example, if the muscles that curl the head forward are weaker than those that pull the head back, then it is harder for your baby to curl her head forward to get her body into a good position for feeding or interacting with you.

What happens as the baby grows? Don't babies need to kick out more?

As your baby enjoys more time awake, she will also enjoy more stretching out, kicking with her legs and waving her arms when you change or dress her, while in the bath, or when you place her on her back on the bed or the floor (with her head supported). Babies learn from these early sensations of moving.

Does putting my baby on her tummy for play help develop control of movements?

Yes, and it is good to start early as this is how neck, shoulder and tummy muscles become stronger. Try for a few minutes at nappy change time or when dressing. You can place your baby on her tummy while she is in your lap or you can lay her on your chest with her face near yours, or even on the floor with your face close to hers. **Remember to always supervise your infant when she spends any time on her tummy.**

Is it OK to put my baby in bouncers or car seats when I am not holding her?

It is generally accepted that placing a baby into a supported seat for short periods of time is OK. A better practice is to carry your baby around with you and when she is tired, place her in her bed to sleep peacefully and soundly in a good position. Often, babies go to sleep while sitting and sleep for less time. Sleep is the biggest consideration, after feeding, for establishing a strong, healthy start to life. Sleep even affects weight gain. Most newborn babies need to go back to sleep after being awake for one and a half hours.[6]

Does being curled in help babies who have been born early or who have had a breech or difficult birth?

Yes, babies who have had these experiences tend to arch and kick, which makes it harder for them to curl in. Helping a baby who has been born early to curl in will help develop the strength of her flexor muscles, which she lacks as a result of missing those last weeks in the uterus. Babies may be irritable and unsettled in the first days and weeks of life after difficult birth experiences.[7] They need help to curl in to become still and calm. (See the Premature Baby section on p. 18 for more detail.)

Knowing ways to help babies help themselves to relax with you in those first days of your baby's life will increase your skills and confidence as a caregiver.

> *For your baby's individual needs and to clarify these ideas, discuss them with your early childhood nurse specialist.*

Quick Tip

Is your baby having difficulty staying calm for feeding and sleeping?

Try wrapping her with a swaddling cloth and lay her on her back. This curled-in posture is the same position she has known for months in your womb. Holding or wrapping your baby in this curled-in posture will help soothe, calm and quiet her.

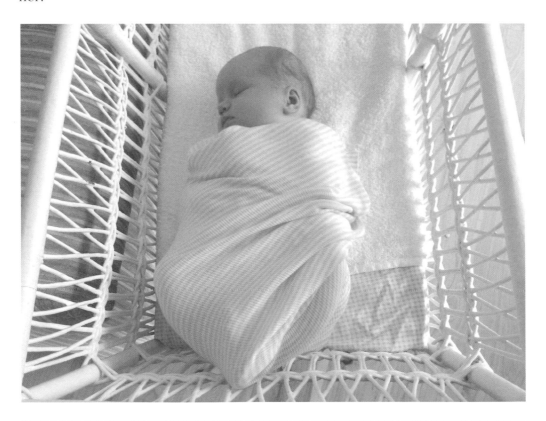

Quick Tip

Being wrapped will help her stay calm as you sit or walk around.

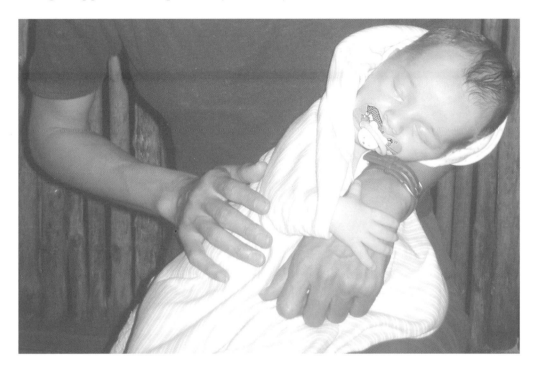

Quick Tip

Curling in helps calm your baby so she is ready to engage with you.

Quick Tip

Still unsettled?

The newborn baby's biggest challenge is learning to handle or regulate all of the information from her new environment. It is so easy for parents to over-stimulate their babies with their enjoyment of holding and talking to them. Learning to read tired signs is a difficult task but will become easier as you get to know your baby. When your little one has had a hard day, she may look tense around the eyes and forehead.

Quick Tip

Try a deep relaxation bath

When the water temperature is just above natural body temperature, your baby will not lose her body heat into the water and will be able to float in this deep bath with your help supporting her head.

Quick Tip

And remember, when your baby is relaxed, awake and calm, it is never too early to start *supervised* tummy time!

> **Key Points**
>
> You can help your baby become calm and settled by wrapping or curling her in your arms when:
> - your baby is starry-eyed (overtired) and difficult to settle, feed or play with
> - carrying her in a sling
> - you need a break, by wrapping and placing her in her cot on her back
> - establishing regular sleep; sleep is the best gift to give your newborn.

The premature baby

This information regarding development is particularly applicable in the early months of the life of a premature baby.[8] The full-term baby, while in the womb, is surrounded by fluid and can move without the pull of gravity, as in a swimming pool. At birth, a full-term baby's flexor muscles are shorter and allow the infant to curl their body in, while a prematurely born infant's body will be less curled.

When babies are born prematurely, the pull of gravity makes it more difficult for them to use their tummy and limb muscles to curl in than when in the womb. These muscles have to work harder and it requires greater effort for these babies to use curling in to calm, feed and interact.

The suggestions in this manual, particularly in the early months following birth, offer ways to help babies to curl in. Parents have found these ideas very useful for their premature infants, particularly in helping their infant to calm, sleep, and eat in those early months. Parents have also found the information in the four-month period helpful to strengthen the tummy and curling in muscles of their infants' limbs for improved success with early movement skills.[9] Researchers report that although most infants born early do develop gross motor skills, many have less strength, balance and coordination, which can affect motor skills and confidence well into the child's future.[10]

Assessing a premature baby's developmental progress becomes more complex as the child grows and changes. Additional help may be a benefit to the premature infant's movement development and other areas such as fine motor skills.

> *We suggest discussing your premature baby's individual needs with your pediatrician, early childhood nurse specialist or a pediatric physiotherapist.*

Notes

[1] L Bly, 'Normal and abnormal development', in D Sekerak Slaton (ed.), *Development of movement in infancy: proceedings*, Division of Physical Therapy, University of North Carolina at Chapel Hill, 1980.

[2] KE Adolph & SA Berger, 'Motor development', in W Damon & R Lerner (series eds) & D Kuhn & RS Siegler (vol. eds), *Handbook of child psychology vol. 2: cognition, perception, and language*, 6th edn, Wiley, New York, 2006, pp. 161–213.

[3] HA Muhiudeen, G Melville-Thomas, SD Ferguson & P Mohan, 'The postures exhibited by 3-day-old full term neonates', *Early Human Development*, vol. 10, nos 1–2, 1984, pp. 57–66.

[4] RG Barr, SJ McMullan, H Spiess, DG Leduc, J Yaremko, R Barfield, TE Francoeur & UA Hunziker, 'Carrying as colic "therapy": a randomized controlled trial', *Pediatrics*, vol. 87, no. 5, 1991, pp. 623–30.

[5] American Academy of Pediatrics Task Force on Sudden Infant Death Syndrome, 'The changing concept of Sudden Infant Death Syndrome: diagnostic coding shifts, controversies regarding the sleeping environment, and new variables to consider in reducing risk', *Pediatrics*, vol. 116, no. 5, 2005, pp. 1245–55. See also http://www.sidsandkids.org.

[6] Department of Families, Housing, Community Services and Indigenous Affairs, 'Recognising tiredness', *Raising Children Network: the Australian parenting website*, 2012, http://raisingchildren.net.au/articles/is_my_child_tired.html/context/731.

[7] R Dolby, B Warren, J Heath, V Meade & G Cooney, 'Developmental care at home: a first year intervention for preterm babies designed to improve self regulation (motor and state) and address parents' concerns', paper presented at the *2nd Annual Perinatal Society meeting of Australia & New Zealand Congress*, 1998.

[8] Dolby et al. 1998.

[9] Dolby et al. 1998.

[10] JF de Kieviet, JP Piek, CS Aarnoudse-Moens & J Oosterlaan, 'Motor development in very preterm and very low-birth-weight children from birth to adolescence: a meta-analysis', *JAMA*, vol. 302, no. 20, 2009, pp. 2235–42.

Chapter 2

Your baby from four to six months

Enjoy the movements your baby is trying to master

Watch and you will observe that from about four months old, your baby has more control over his body and will be able to look at and play with you more readily. When he holds his body still and his head centred in the middle of his body, he can practise looking directly at you and can connect more with you and the outside world. He is just beginning to realise he can make things happen. He smiles at you and you smile back! This discovery can be enjoyed in play and by 'talking' with you. Notice how your baby practices becoming more excited, yet is still able to calm down with your help.[1]

What your baby is working on

Your baby is strengthening both the muscle groups that curl in and those that stretch out. This will give him more control over moving his body, arms and legs. Observe his increased control in each of the following illustrations.

Sit your baby on your lap while he is awake and content and you will notice he is starting to look around more and more, especially if you give him as much support as he needs around the middle of his body. He may also try to reach out to touch a person or a toy if he has enough support from you.

When you lay your baby on his back you will notice he tries to bring his legs up into the air so that he can sometimes touch his hands to his knees, which strengthens his tummy muscles.

If you show him a toy, he will follow it with his eyes …

and may even try to touch it. Notice his active, pursed mouth as he concentrates …

and brings it into his mouth to explore. His mouth is a terrific third hand! Mouthing toys will also help your baby learn to form consonant sounds.[2]

If you help your baby to roll from his back onto his tummy, wait as he tries to lift his head clear of the floor when on his side.

He is developing strong neck muscles, which will help him to hold his head steady so he can use his eyes to watch and see well in all positions.

Finish with the roll you have just tried, so your baby can now experience the tummy position.

You may notice he is just starting to stay in this position, but it is still hard for him to lift his head very high off the ground to look around, particularly if he has not had much experience in tummy time. Babies who sleep on their backs like to spend time awake on their backs. Your baby will depend on you to help him get stronger on his tummy through practice.

He may try to look at a toy and use his eyes to follow the toy from side to side, again depending on his head and back muscle strength while on his tummy.

While your baby is on his back, gently pull him up to sitting, and observe as he holds his head steady as you move him. What great neck muscles!

His back may still be weak and slouch a little while he tries to sit.

It is easier to hold your baby in standing because he is becoming stronger on his legs. He will become even stronger with your help to practise!

Now lift up and fly your baby in the air by holding him under his chest.

He will enjoy this game and show his pleasure by moving his legs. Notice his increasing strength in holding up his head so he can look around.

Each of these positions helps your baby to build the strength in his muscles and allows him to experiment with moving more. All the movements are fun games!

> *Strength and practice are the two most important areas researchers have found to make movements efficient[3], so babies wiggle less and calm themselves more easily.*

How Mum and Dad can help

You can help your baby develop the balance between muscles that curl in and those that stretch out. The balanced use of these muscles helps your baby to hold his body in a steady posture as he sits on your lap and later, begins to sit alone.

Make sure your baby is well-supported in your arms when he sits on your lap. A well-supported sitting position helps him to hold his body still so it is easier to look and pay attention to the world around him. This is the first step to the skills of attending to and learning.

Increase tummy time with push-ups to help prepare your baby for getting ready to move forward on the floor. Increasing tummy time will also help to prevent the back of his head becoming flat. If your baby's head is very flat it is hard for him to look to both sides when lying down.

> *If your baby's strength does not improve with extra tummy time, be sure to see your early childhood nurse specialist for their opinion.*

Some questions you might ask about the four- to six-month period

Why observe a baby's movement skills before he has developed any milestones such as rolling or crawling?

The average infant has many movement skills which begin to develop at four months of age. These skills will prepare him to take in more information, by reaching out and initiating with his eyes, with his voice and with his hands, months before his movements (such as rolling at about six months, crawling at about eight to nine months and walking at about one year of age). As a parent, you can become more aware of these developing movement skills through observation. Sometimes professionals trained in movement development may be able to offer you ideas for supporting your baby if he is finding movement a bit too hard.

My baby doesn't like playing on his tummy for very long. Is this normal?

Being happy during tummy time is a skill which usually emerges between four and six months of age. You may notice your baby being much happier on his tummy as he reaches his fourth month. Being able to lift up his head, which is very big and heavy, depends on the balance of muscles which are now developing. Your baby will not like this position until he can look around and support some weight on his arms, which makes the tummy position a lot less work. You can support your baby's efforts by helping to roll him from his back—his usual position—to his tummy, as described in the Quick Tip at the end of this section. In this way your infant will have the joy of experiencing this movement for himself and he will be happier staying on his tummy.

What is the best toy for my baby?

The best toy is your face. You may notice that very soon after birth, your baby tries to focus and study faces of the important people in his life. By four months, he is more advanced with his study of your face and is now also studying your voice and mouth. He will soon begin to attract your attention to him by using his voice, in the same way that you attract his attention to you. Support your infant by looking, smiling and talking to him as much as possible.

How do I help my baby get ready for sitting?

Parents often notice that between four and six months, babies start to sit forward on their bottoms when put into sitting and sometimes think that they are ready to sit alone. However, the muscles that work the pelvic area are just starting to function together—another emerging skill. These muscles will not be working well enough to support the upper body for several more months.

Your baby will be happier and will not need to work as hard if his upper body continues to be supported in an inclined chair between the ages of four and six months. In a supported position, he can use his hands for developing his reaching skills, instead of needing to use them to stay balanced and not fall over while sitting. It is very hard to know when a sitting baby is tired, and it is easy to overdo sitting. Until he is strong enough in his shoulder and back muscles to get out of sitting by going onto his tummy, your child will be more successful and happier in supported sitting.

My baby loves to stand up. Is this OK? Should I be using walkers or Jolly Jumpers with him?

You will notice how excited your baby becomes when stood on his feet, which shows how much he enjoys this position. A baby between four and six months of age will support some weight on his legs when standing, but his little legs collapse when tired. Although you may have a walker or a Jolly Jumper, the best option is for your baby to stand with you. Standing in your lap with your arms around him is just the right amount of support to make standing a fun experience at this young age, and in your arms he will give you good signals of when he becomes tired so that you will be able to put him down. We discourage the use of walkers and jumpers because babies are learning from the movements they make by themselves and standing in walkers encourages different muscles to be used to stand, delaying the development of crawling skills by several months.

How do babies begin to communicate at this age?

We all need to trust others. Support your developing relationship with your baby by starting a game. You might make a sound and then wait for your baby to take his turn to make a sound, which you then repeat. This is the start of conversation.

Sometimes he may need more time to respond to your voice or your play, so exaggerate your expressions, and just wait. You will notice your baby start to imitate or 'mirror' what you do, using facial expressions, sounds or waving his arms. Take care to always be ready to comfort and not overwhelm your baby during play. If he becomes too stimulated, you will see him look away from you, which helps him relax and calm down. This is the way your baby takes a break.

Not very strong on his tummy yet? Play the 'roly-poly' game at nappy changing times.

You can play games to help strengthen your baby's tummy muscles.[4] Try this when he is facing you while lying on the change table, your lap or the floor. Take his hips while he is on his back and roll him from side to side. Wait until he completes the roll and ends up on his tummy for a quick push-up, then you can help him roll onto his back for another turn!

Key Points

- Encourage your baby to practise when you help him roll onto his tummy, do little push-ups and get stronger.
- You are your baby's favourite toy! Talk to him, read to him and imitate his sounds.
- Stand him in your arms and don't use walkers or Jolly Jumpers.
- Keep sleeping and feeding as your baby's most important tasks.

If you have any questions, please ask your early childhood nurse specialist to go through the Meade Movement Checklist (MMCL)[5] with you to understand what your baby is working on and how best to help. Researchers have found this set of movements to be very predictive to how well your child will do in his future.[6]

Notes

1   R Dolby, B Warren, J Heath, V Meade & G Cooney, 'Developmental care at home: a first year intervention for preterm babies designed to improve self regulation (motor and state) and address parents' concerns', paper presented at the *2nd Annual Perinatal Society meeting of Australia & New Zealand Congress*, 1998.

2   JM Iverson, 'Developing language in a developing body: the relationship between motor development and language development', *Journal of Child Language*, vol. 37, no. 2, 2010, pp. 229–61.

3   HA Muhiudeen, G Melville-Thomas, SD Ferguson & P Mohan, 'The postures exhibited by 3-day-old full term neonates', *Early Human Development*, vol. 10, nos 1–2, 1984, pp. 57–66.

4   Dolby et al. 1998.

5   V Meade, *The Meade Movement Checklist*, 1980, video recording, Port Macquarie. Distributed through www.vickiemeade.com.

6   VA Meade, JK Sweeney, LS Chandler & BJ Woodward, 'Identifying 4-month-old infants at-risk in community screening', *Pediatric Physical Therapy*, vol. 21, no. 2, 2009, pp. 150–7.

Chapter 3

Your baby from six to eight months

Enjoy the movements your baby has mastered

Your baby has made great progress. She is now able to balance her curling-in and stretching-out muscles. This allows her to take control of her body and hold her arms and legs still when she needs to. She can now centre her body when you hold her in a sitting or standing position and she will be getting ready to start moving through her own experimentation and practice.

What your baby is working on

Your baby is becoming more stable in different positions and will soon start moving away from you. But she will want to stop to look back at you and be reassured that you are still there. At the same time, as she starts to sit on her own, she will also want to be with you for longer times in play and interaction.

Your six-month-old-baby is strong! When she sits in your lap, she will actively reach out to grab any object she can see. Notice that you need to give her less support because she holds her body so much straighter.

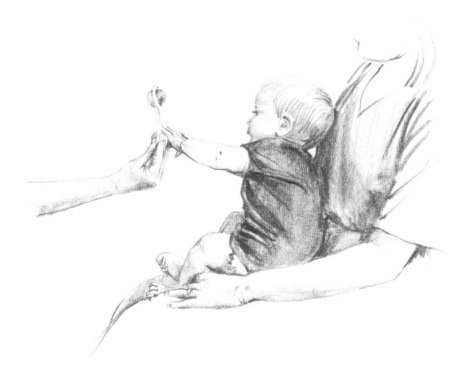

Notice too the beautiful outstretched arm and fingers as she reaches out into space while on your lap, but doesn't lose her balance. She can easily turn her head from side to side to follow all the activity in her world. Her new strength in sitting will also help her to form new and different sounds in her mouth![1]

Place your baby on the floor and you will see how easily your six-month-old can play on her tummy.

She has become strong over the past two months and can easily hold her head high as she looks around and watches you, so she doesn't mind this position now. The stronger your baby is, the higher she will push her chest off the ground. This strength comes from hours and hours of push-up practice, which she started to enjoy at about four months through all the tummy time play you gave her.

Depending on your baby's strength on her tummy, she will start to move her body from side to side and balance on one arm to reach out and touch a toy. All her experiments with moving on her tummy will help her develop her crawling skills.

Look at those fingers stretch! This strong baby can support her body on one arm as her eyes focus intently on the apple rattle.

Sometimes the movements your baby tries while on her tummy may mean she loses her balance, so she rolls onto her back. Losing balance is a very important step in motor development as it gives the baby movement sensations, a critical component of sensory–motor development.[2] She will not want to stay long on her back and will make every effort to roll onto her side to get back to her tummy.

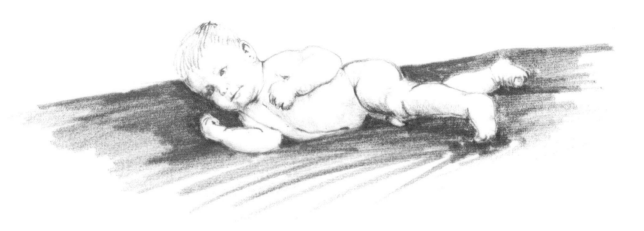

Notice how strongly she can lift her head up off the floor as she manoeuvers over onto her tummy to play.

Her ease of moving from back to tummy results from all your 'roly-poly' play at four months, when you helped her to roll from side to side and she ended up over on her tummy.

You may notice the biggest change is while sitting. Your baby will now try to sit alone without leaning forward to put her hands on the floor. It is hard work and requires a good balance of strength in both the muscles of the back and the tummy, which support her head in a good position to see. Eventually her sitting will improve so that she can reach out and use both hands to play instead of using her hands for balance. This sitting posture also gives her a chance to push air out from her tummy and make louder and more varied sounds as a step to speaking.[3]

You will also notice a big change in strength when you play 'flying' with your baby. Watch as she stretches her legs high up into the air. The muscles of her hips have become strong with play on her tummy and standing in your lap over the past two months.

Each of these positions helps your baby to build the strength in her muscles, which allows her to experiment with moving by herself. Her growing strength and many opportunities for practice in all these positions sets the stage for the eight- to twelve-month period of moving around on the floor and getting into standing by herself.

How Mum and Dad can help

You can increase floor time for more tummy play so your baby's shoulders and arms build up strength. It also helps to increase play time in all other positions, such as while she is sitting on your lap, pulling to sit, standing and flying. This helps your baby experience the sensations of movement and strengthens her back muscles—a baby gym workout! Researchers know from comparing different cultures that the more parents exercise their babies, the better the babies develop motor skills.[4]

When we try something new, we all need confidence. As your baby starts to move, you help her to become confident. She will look at you as she moves away to be reassured that you are still there if she needs you. If your baby feels reassured, she will continue to play with the toy or crawl further away for more adventure. If feeling scared or insecure, she may cry, meaning, 'Mum! Dad! I need you!' She is asking for more reassurance or encouragement, or even direct help from you.

It is important too that you help your baby learn safety as she begins to explore. For example, help her avoid power points and sharp objects with your firm 'No!' as you move her to safer ground.[5]

Babies enjoy simple play of one thing at a time to concentrate on, and they love the same thing over and over! When your baby is busy in her own play, try to let her be alone for a few minutes.

As you imitate your baby's increasing number of sounds and facial expressions, exaggerate your response and wait ... you will be rewarded as your baby repeats after you again and again. Take turns and allow your baby time to respond while still respecting natural pauses in play. Now you are having conversations!

Some questions you might ask about the six- to eight-month period

Is it normal that my baby still doesn't like being on her tummy?

There are many babies who just do not like tummy time! It takes a lot of work to hold her head up and look around, and as your baby becomes stronger at sitting, she may prefer this as an easier position to see and interact with you and her world.

Is there a better way to help her learn to crawl?

She will still enjoy the roly-poly game, so try it again to give her more time to learn to roll over onto her tummy by herself; then she can build up strength on her tummy in her own time. Try the exercise in the Quick Tip on p. 45 to give her more chances to build up strength in each shoulder as she learns to get herself into sitting, an often preferred place to be!

Does it hurt my baby to skip crawling?

There are many paths that babies can take in their development. Some prefer to roll around the house, others to scoot on their bottoms before pulling to stand and walking away. Any time on her tummy will help your baby to learn a way to crawl around, so if you would like your baby to crawl, it does help to keep trying.[6] It is thought that crawling may help with shoulder strength for future ball and writing skills, and it opens up amazing opportunities for her to explore and interact with you. Crawling also influences the developing communication skills.[7]

My baby just wants to 'walk' all the time with my help.

Babies love to be on their feet. This is another time in development when movement is closely linked to arousal. Babies get a buzz out of standing! It is wonderful as one movement experience, but it is nice for your baby to get a full range and to experience movements she can do on her own. Remember to choose standing options other than walkers or Jolly Jumpers to create the best range of movements for your baby's future skill development. Your baby needs to experiment on her own to build strength, balance and coordination.

Is it normal that my baby doesn't want to play alone but always wants me to carry her around?

At six months, your baby is having a love affair with you! You will notice she will try to 'kiss' you by getting close and sucking on your face or chin. It is a wonderful time, although tiring. Try to be patient and enjoy the adoration as independent play skills will be developing soon. Your baby will get better at playing alone as she learns to use her body to move around. She will be steadier while sitting and be able to direct her arms and fingers to get toys more easily.

Quick Tip

Still not keen on her tummy? Try this!

Hold your baby in the middle of her body. Roll her onto one side so she can put one arm onto the floor. Move slowly so she can help to sit herself up. This is an easier version of a push-up and can build shoulder strength one arm at a time.[8] Plus she will end up in a sitting position, a rewarding place to be! Be sure to do to both sides.

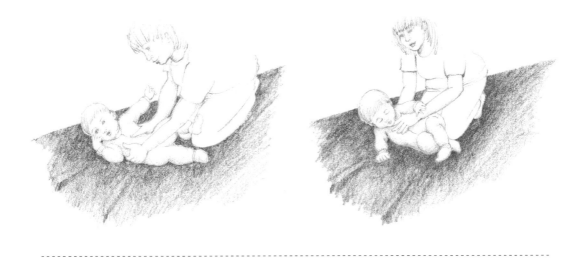

Key Points

- Your baby now has all the big muscles needed to move herself around.
- Keep offering a full range of practice opportunities including roly-poly, tummy time, sitting and standing to help all the muscles become strong.
- Movement and sounds are closely connected; movements help sounds to develop.
- Imitate all the sounds your baby makes and soon she will be saying words.

Notes

[1] JM Iverson, 'Developing language in a developing body: the relationship between motor development and language development', *Journal of Child Language*, vol. 37, no. 2, 2010, pp. 229–61.

[2] KE Adolph & SA Berger, 'Motor development', in W Damon & R Lerner (series eds) & D Kuhn & RS Siegler (vol. eds), *Handbook of child psychology vol. 2: cognition, perception, and language*, 6th edn, Wiley, New York, 2006, pp. 161–213.

[3] Iverson, 2010.

[4] LB Karasik, KE Adolph, CS Tamis-LeMonda & M Bornstein, 'WEIRD walking: cross-cultural research on motor development', *Behavior and Brain Sciences*, vol. 33, nos 2–3, 2010, pp. 95–6.

[5] LB Karasik, CS Tamis-LeMonda, KE Adolph & KA Dimitropoulou, 'How mothers encourage and discourage infants' motor actions', *Infancy*, vol. 13, no. 4, 2008, pp. 366–92.

[6] Adolph & Berger, 2006.

[7] Iverson, 2010.

[8] V Meade, *Partners in movement: a family centered approach to pediatric kinesiology*, Vickie Meade, 2008. Available at www.vickiemeade.com.

Chapter 4

Your baby from eight to twelve months

Look at me! I have mastered using my big muscles

Between eight and twelve months of age, depending on your baby's individual temperament and personality, he will start to use the building blocks of muscles he has been strengthening all this time.

Your active baby is trying to move around and explore his world. This is an exciting time for him. Together you will continue to build on the two-way communication and the two-way trusting relationship you have been developing.

What your baby is working on

Your baby works hard to be stable in every position. Being stable means it is easy for him to change positions and not fall over too often. He will be more confident and adventurous as he becomes more willing to try new movement skills. Your baby's goal is to pull himself up so he can stand as he holds onto furniture or objects.

If you place your baby on his back to change him, he will quickly roll over to get into a position to move. Notice the active hands and feet!

He wants to get into positions to play or move. Admire his strong arms as he pushes himself into sitting. Notice one leg is tucked under the body as he moves.

Getting into sitting independently allows him freedom of choice to move, play or both. All his previous tummy time experience has made his arms and back strong.

And … that toy! Notice how your baby connects eyes to hands with his active reach sideways towards the toy.

He is able to move his whole body sideways to touch the toy he wants … and watch his little toes as he actively pushes his whole body forward.

Look at that reach! Experimenting in each position allows your baby to learn how far he can go before he falls and challenges his developing senses, strength, coordination and balance. This is critical for the growth of future skills.

Watch him try to bring both knees under him so his hand is free to grab the toy.

You will notice him experimenting for hours trying to strengthen and coordinate, rocking and rolling, holding himself up on his arms and knees, until … success! Moving forward at last! Place something in his path and he will go right over it.

The rhythmical movements of rocking often seen before a new stage also start the mouth rocking and rolling with new sounds![1]

Once your baby starts to move he will be driven to pull himself up onto any object that will hold his weight.

Notice how easily he holds on even with open hands and pushes with his feet to get his legs underneath him. Once standing, he starts to experiment with reaching and adjusting his balance on his feet. Observe his active toes when he is on his feet.

It will now take months of experimentation with standing before your baby will be ready to take off with a step or two.

Enjoy watching how dexterous he is with his emerging balance skills! He will walk sideways, letting go with one hand to cross gaps. He will try to push anything that moves or comes into his path, and will try to get himself back down to the floor without falling onto his bottom too often.

How Mum and Dad can help

Practice makes perfect

Movement development is very much like emotional and communication development. Parents are extremely influential, first because of their awareness of just what their baby is trying to do and then just by being with and enjoying each thing their infant is trying. Researchers have found that parents often don't know exactly what their baby could be doing at each age and often ask the child to try too much or too little.[2]

You are powerful! Developing your two-way movement relationship with your baby depends on your awareness. Enjoy and be the cheer squad for each move he tries, even if he ends up falling. He tried! And it will be this practice that makes the difference.

At the same time, continue to show him safe limits. In learning these skills, your baby will practise his persistence by calming himself and trying again. This is the self-control of emotion and physical enjoyment we all strive for.

Some questions you might ask about the eight- to twelve-month period

Does it matter that my baby still only likes to sit and not move around?

Babies are individuals and have different likes and desires. Your baby may enjoy looking, socialising, making sounds and using his hands. Sometimes it is difficult for him to get to a point where he is strong enough on his tummy to move around. Try the Quick Tip on p. 56 as another way to experiment while he is sitting.

How do I help my baby, who is just starting to get strong on his tummy, learn to crawl?

Try to give him as many opportunities to be on his tummy while he talks to you and plays with you. With enough time, he will try to move his arms to reach out to you or to toys, and will learn more about how his body moves while in this position. Learning about his body will make it easier for him to enjoy all the time it takes to learn to move around.

How do I help my baby learn how to sit up by himself?

You can help by using the Quick Tip at the end of the six-to-eight-month chapter (see p. 45), which involves rolling your baby to one side and waiting for him to help push himself up using one arm. Or you can set him down onto one side of his body, as illustrated by the Quick Tip at the end of this chapter. Both methods help challenge your baby's balance so he can learn more about how his body moves into different positions.

Does it matter if my child just prefers to be in a walker for long periods during the day?

Standing and walking are exciting movements for your baby. However, walkers are discouraged by most healthcare providers, particularly if the walker has wheels and could become unsafe. Also, too much time spent walking limits the development of other skills which are important for developing independence. Strength, balance and coordination develop when your child is moving under his own steam.

Does it mean my baby is ready to walk when he pulls himself up on furniture?

When your child pulls himself up on furniture, he does not yet have a very good sense of his balance and how his legs are connected to the rest of him. This will come as he has the chance to experiment in this position. Watch as he tries to figure out how to bend his legs to get back down, to walk sideways (cruise) along furniture and eventually, as he feels steadier, to let go and stand alone. Once he has spent time learning where he is in space, he will take off with steps of his own making.

When will he start walking on his own?

Most babies start taking steps at around one year of age, but this can vary from eight months to fifteen months. Development differs according to each child, and so many factors influence when they feel ready to let go and take off on their own. (See Chapter 5 for more detail.)

Quick Tip

Is your baby so good at sitting, he doesn't want to explore moving?

Try this 'set down'. Each time you go to place him on the floor, set him to one side so his arm comes down to the floor first.[3] This will encourage him to continue the movement onto his tummy or to get himself back into a sitting position.

> ## Key Points
>
> You encourage your baby to grow in his movements when you:
> - are aware of each little movement your baby is practising
> - give lots of time and praise during play
> - reward every sound by repeating it, waiting for his turn and repeating the sound again
> - create obstacles for your baby to crawl over using your legs or pillows
> - let your baby experiment in standing by encouraging cruising around furniture
> - keep your baby safe.

Notes

[1] JM Iverson, 'Developing language in a developing body: the relationship between motor development and language development', *Journal of Child Language*, vol. 37, no. 2, 2010, pp. 229–61.

[2] KE Adolph & SA Berger, 'Motor development', in W Damon & R Lerner (series eds) & D Kuhn & RS Siegler (vol. eds), *Handbook of child psychology vol. 2: cognition, perception, and language*, 6th edn, Wiley, New York, 2006, pp. 161–213.

[3] V Meade, *Partners in movement: a family centered approach to pediatric kinesiology*, Vickie Meade, 2008. Available at www.vickiemeade.com.

Chapter 5

Every baby is different

What you and your baby have achieved

By twelve months of age or shortly afterwards, your baby will pull up to stand on two feet! For one year, your baby has worked hard to achieve this position and she will feel very excited and pleased with herself.

Enjoy what you and your baby have achieved together. You have helped your baby safely arrive from your arms to stand on two feet and look around at the world in the same way you do.

She has mastered the strengthening and balancing of muscle groups which form the basis of all the new movements to come in the next few years: walking, bending over for toys, squatting, climbing, running and jumping. The opportunities you have offered for practice are priceless. Your child will build on these basic skills and may enjoy a sport as she grows older. You now understand how to help, enjoy and be a part of your child's progress. Congratulations to you both!

Integrating communication skills into your play

At each of the ages discussed so far, your baby has been experimenting with sound. From the first cries that call you during the newborn period to the 'oohs' of delight at playing with you at four months and the increasing range of sounds as posture improves during sitting and standing, your baby is asking you to have 'conversations'.

Now that your baby is experimenting while standing, you will notice more vocal play with more sounds in different combinations. Researchers now understand that the motor and communication systems are closely linked both in the brain and in experiences. When your baby experiments with rocking and waving, the sounds she is making tend to be repeated more and more often and in unison with movement.[1]

From the first days of her life, she was comforted when you spoke gently to her. Talking in a quiet, reassuring manner and explaining everything that you were doing in the early months helped her learn about you, and to understand that you were about to bath, feed or soothe her after excitement or were just playing with sounds.

Next, showing your baby coloured books as she seemed curious about them (perhaps as early as four months of age) helped her become interested in reading years before she would start herself. Pointing to and talking about the pictures you showed her, watching for any response and then repeating her sounds increased her interest in you and sounds.

Now your baby's movements support an increase in the number and variety of different sounds that she will form into words with your help. Your early efforts set the stage and now you will enjoy her first words, either in sound or in gestures, like 'No!'

As she nears twelve months of age, her movements will also be used in gestures for words she cannot yet say. Another major step to putting words together into sentences can happen as early as eighteen months of age when she combines a word and a gesture![2]

Each baby achieves motor skills on their own pathway

Each baby is a unique individual who has a different way of knowing, sensing and exploring the world. Progress through the sequence of building blocks of movement depends on a combination of experience, strength and your baby's personality, plus many other factors within each child and her environment.

The time it takes a baby to achieve standing will vary

Some babies will stand well before twelve months (even as young as seven months) while other infants may take up to fifteen months to stand.[3] This difference will depend on each individual child's strength, interest, motivation, willingness to explore and opportunities to practise, practise, practise.

Each of us has a combination of factors which affect how our motor skills develop. Natural motor skills vary; some of us can be seen as born athletes. Quick balance reflexes, natural strength, good muscle tone (degree of firmness of our muscles), our body's build and our mental awareness (which include our sense of the position of our body in space) are unique to each of us. These factors combine with emotional development and motivation. Each individual uses all these factors with a willingness to take risks using her body. As we grow and develop sporting interests, the opportunity to practise can influence skills in one who may not find it as easy as the born athlete.

It is the same for babies as it is for us. Practice can make all the difference. And the difference can matter if the child grows older and still cannot master the basic building blocks.

When does taking time matter?

If your baby is content and enjoying each step, then taking longer may meet your baby's needs. Some infants who sit for long periods of time may become very good at using their hands and eyes together during play and are happy. If during any stage your baby becomes more demanding and does not seem happy lying or sitting or playing with a toy, there are ways to help.

The tips given in this guide support your baby's efforts at each stage, however, if time is passing and your baby seems discontented or you have concerns, she may need to be checked by your early childhood nurse specialist or your doctor.

Some babies do not like frustration and can be shown an easier way. Parents might see their baby as 'not trying' or being 'lazy'. Babies have a built-in, natural urge to move and to become independent, so moving before they have mastered the next stage may seem too hard to them. Pediatric physiotherapists and occupational therapists can suggest simple ways to help your baby enjoy moving. Some babies may benefit from or need extra help along the way, due to being born early or having birth difficulties.

Conclusion

We hope you have enjoyed this guide to the challenges your baby faces in each of the four stages during her first year.

Your baby has learned to help calm herself, with your assistance, in the newborn period. By four to six months, your baby is working hard to strengthen her body in different positions against gravity, and is dependent on your help in putting her in different positions, particularly for time on her tummy.

You have observed the developing strength of your baby's muscles over the months, until, after hours of practice and your encouragement, she begins to move under her own steam. With this movement comes new opportunities for her to explore her environment, to use her hands to explore new objects, and to use her mouth in different positions to explore new sounds. All with your help, awareness, encouragement and patience. Again, congratulations!

Notes

[1] JM Iverson, 'Developing language in a developing body: the relationship between motor development and language development', *Journal of Child Language*, vol. 37, no. 2, 2010, pp. 229–61.

[2] JM Iverson, 'Multimodality in infancy: vocal–motor and speech–gesture coordinations in typical and atypical development', *Enfance*, vol. 2010, no. 3, pp. 257–74.

[3] MC Piper & J Darrah, *Motor assessment of the developing infant*, WB Saunders, Philadelphia, 1994.